Play it again, Sam

PLAY IT AGAIN, SAM

Sam McAughtry

Illustrations by
Dermie Seymour

Blackstaff Press

Published by Blackstaff Press Limited, 255A Upper Newtownards Road, Belfast BT4 3JF.

ISBN 0 85640 176 5

Printed in Ireland by Cahill 1976 Limited.

Contents

All these stories, with the exception of 'Come on Kaye Don!' and 'A Pound of Steak for Stuffing', have been broadcast on 'Sunday Miscellany' on RTE. 'Come on Kaye Don!' has been broadcast by BBC Northern Ireland. 'A Pound of Steak for Stuffing' and 'Tired of Life' have been published in the *Ulster Tatler*.

Tired of Life

In the spring of 1929 I decided to run away from home. I was eight years of age. It must have been spring because the grass was damp during running away hours, and the reason I know the grass was damp is that I had resolved to sit on the damp grass on purpose, after running away, get the cold and sicken and die, and teach my mother a thorough-going lesson for what she had done to me. Which was as follows:

I was standing at the door of our house in Cosgrave street when Davy McAuley and Frankie Pattison walked past.

'Where are you going?' I asked them.

'We're going to Joe's,' they said, 'are you coming?'

They meant the picture house owned by a man called Joe McKibbin. A pleasure palace where, for a penny, you could occupy twelve inches of wooden form, breathe in concentrated disinfectant, and scream at the antics of Charlie Chaplin, or Buster Keaton, or a hundred other heroes.

But I hadn't any pennies. In the circumstances Plan X was indicated.

'I'm not going to the pictures,' I shouted at the

top of my voice. 'I've no money, and my mother won't give me a penny.'

The plan worked perfectly at the start. Before I had even closed my mouth the kitchen door was flung open, a soapy hand came out, and I was hauled inside the house, coming to rest by the washtub where mother spent most of her waking hours. I tensed myself for the sudsy slap across the back of the leg. Sure enough it arrived. Then Plan X allowed for a tongue-lashing for showing mother up in front of the neighbours, and this, too, arrived on schedule. The last part of the calculation foresaw a penny being crammed into my hand and myself being hurled back outside again, to set off with my mates to the pictures.

Not so. All I got was hurled outside. No penny. No nothing. I made up my mind to run away.

Up Cosgrave Street, up the Limestone Road, and into Alexandra Park. There I sat deliberately on the damp grass in order to kill myself.

After about three minutes I was beginning to think it wasn't the greatest way to go. I rose, pulled my trousers away from the skin, and decided instead to climb up and touch the screen the next time I went to the pictures. Everybody knew the screen was full of electricity. I could shout at the horrified audience: 'This is my mother's fault,' and then touch the screen.

I was interrupted in my planning by a voice, calling me: 'D'ye want to see a bird's nest?'

It was a boy from the Limestone Road district. He beckoned me over to a hawthorn brush. Sure enough there was a nest, round and snug. But it was empty.

I tensed myself for the sudsy slap across the back of the leg.

9

'Don't touch it,' the boy warned me, 'or they won't come back to it. They can smell if you touch it.'

We stared at it for a bit and then wandered down to the almost deserted swings, occupying one each.

'What school do you go to?' the other asked.

'Barney's,' I told him, giving him the nickname of St Barnabas'.

'I go to the Star of the Sea,' he said.

I looked at him with interest. 'What's it like?' I wanted to know.

'Rotten,' he replied, 'you get hit with the tawse for nothing.'

'We get hit with the cane for nothing,' I said. 'Last week I got six slaps just for climbing up a spout. Barney's is stinking,' I told him, with feeling. But there was something I wanted this fellow to clear up. 'Tell me this,' I asked him, 'do you have to drink holy water in the Star of the Sea?'

My companion turned round on his swing and looked at me as if was ready to be certified. 'You don't drink holy water,' he said patiently, 'are you stupid or something?'

Before I could pursue the matter any further the other boy jumped off his swing and, giving himself a two-length start, challenged me to a race over to the river.

The river was actually a narrow stream. It was full of spricks. Off came our slippers to be shoved in our pockets, and we began to co-operate in the catching of spricks. Working as a skilled team we surrounded and scooped up a good dozen spricks, letting them off again because we had no jampot to keep them in. As the afternoon wore on we gradually worked our way upstream until we had reached the point where it emerged in Alexandra Park after its journey under the Antrim Road from the Corporation Waterworks. When we were too cold to stand it any longer we rubbed each other's toes with grass to warm them up, then we put our canvas slippers back on again.

'I go home this way,' the boy from the Limestone Road said, pointing to a hole in the boundary hedge where thousands of boys before him had punched an entrance to the Antrim Road. He turned back to me before he left: 'Will you be here tomorrow?' he asked.

'I don't know,' I told him. 'I might kill myself. But if I don't,' I finished, 'I'll see you beside the bird's nest after school.'

Then I went on my way home. The family were all sitting up to the tea when I walked in. Without interrupting their eating they moved up to make room for me.

I couldn't help thinking whenever I sat down at the table that not one of them had even noticed that I had run away and returned again. I decided to run away properly the next day. Either that or deliberately choke myself to death with bread and butter.

The Great Paper Race

Times have certainly changed as far as newsboys are concerned. Selling papers is an honourable way of earning a few bob now. The neighbours don't mind. Boys belonging to the top-dog families in the district shove the paper through your letter box now, and nobody thinks any the less of them.

I'll tell you one thing: it wasn't like that forty or fifty years ago. At least not in our family anyway.

My mother ruled with an iron hand on this issue. She didn't allow any of her boys to sell papers. She reckoned it made a showbox out of her. Even though we hadn't two halfpennies to scratch ourselves with my mother placed newsboys alongside of gypsies in the social scale.

As far as I can remember the rest of my brothers weren't interested. But I was, and that's for sure. Selling papers was one of the most exciting activities I could imagine, you see. I disobeyed mother every chance I got.

For me Saturday night was when it all happened. Up on the Antrim Road near the New Lodge Road there was a supply point where the paper boys picked up the *Ireland's Saturday Night*, Belfast's sporting paper, or the *Ulster*, as it's called to this

12

day. Anything up to the length of thirty men and boys would be assembled, when up would jingle the pony and cart loaded to the top with papers. As soon as it stopped the newsboys would push and shove something desperate to get their papers, for speed was money, and the whole idea was to be first into virgin territory. The vanman would thrust bundles into upstretched hands and grab the payment as he did so. It was a penny to buy and three halfpence to sell. Then away the pony would gallop, but it wouldn't move any quicker than the newsboys, I'll tell you that much. They would scoot towards the four points of the compass, shouting their heads off as they ran.

Naturally I hadn't any standing order for papers, but what I did have was a one-sided arrangement with one of the most long-suffering and tolerant characters in Tiger's Bay — Fat Kerrigan. Fat was my own age. He wasn't just *allowed* to sell papers — he was *directed* to sell them by his mother, for his old man was out of work. I used to think Fat Kerrigan was steeped in luck. But I liked him very much as well, for he would always let me sell some of his papers for him.

When the papers arrived I would be standing back from the crowd. Fat Kerrigan would plunge right into the action when the cart drew up, and in seconds he would burst back out again, shaking newsboys off him as he did, pushing towards me like an icebreaker, five dozen *Ulsters* under his arm. Reaching me he would whip off six of them and hand them to me.

'See you here at half eight,' he would say, giving me one hour. 'Try and not get stewed,' Fat would shout, as he took off, jet propelled.

Now this business about being stewed wasn't anything to do with the beer, for we were only about eleven at the time. No. When you were stewed you were left with papers under your arm that nobody wanted. Circulation managers'll know the feeling.

The truth of the matter was that I would be having a pretty good night if I managed to sell three of my six papers. But no matter. Fat would get rid of them, even should he knock doors and offer them at a halfpenny each to do it.

Anyway I was off and away, filled with a wild excitement. Now I had a passport to magnificent places. I could hop on to moving trams and run upstairs with no thick ear from the conductor. Sometimes — oh, the bliss of it! — I would see one of my mates on the tram, travelling as a fare-paying passenger. I would wink at him. An urchin's wink. A newsboy's wink. Like the Artful Dodger. 'Second-er-Ulster' I would shout to a tramful of people who had nearly finished reading it already. My eyes would be sideways on the mate, relishing his envy.

Everybody liked paper boys on Saturday nights. You were allowed into the pubs. The lovely marvellous pubs, with their rich, brown mahogany and their splendid mirrors and gleaming brass. Labourers in their good suits were in there, uncharacteristically relaxed, and confident. Men patted you on the head, and the publican watched you warily in case you tried it on with the more fuddled customers. Everybody in the pub already had their papers when I got there, but never mind. I was in there with all that lovely, noisy, grown up, forbidden atmosphere. It was heaven, that's what it was. All of Rockefeller's millions couldn't have purchased from me that one glorious hour each fairy-lit Belfast Saturday night.

It was the minister who finally put an end to it: the rector of our church. He was a passenger on one of the trams that I boarded. I was waving the paper right under his face before I recognised him.

Now I would probably have got away with it if I'd just wished him the time of day politely, headed off, and left it at that. But no. I have to be razor-sharp with the reflexes. The minute I recognised the Reverend Patterson I have to say: 'You didn't see Fat Kerrigan, did you, sir? He dropped these, and I'm trying to catch him to give them back.'

Imagine. What a daft thing to say. The Reverend Patterson nearly killed himself laughing on the spot. Worse than that, he called at our house the next day to visit Mother, for I must have put her into his head, and during his visit he laughed at what a lively character I was and he was sure Mother had an entertaining time with me around.

Well, I've already told you about Mother's iron hand. More like tungsten steel, it was. Especially round the legs. No more papers for Sam.

Mind you, a lot of years later I was back at the papers again. But that was only writing for them. There's no comparison. Give me selling papers any time...

The Mutton Dummies

It was certainly a great surprise to me when Herbie Beattie asked me to his party.

Herbie was a great mate of mine. We sat together in the public elementary school where we got what passed for a schooling forty years ago. He was good looking, with fair hair in tight waves, snub nose, and good shoulders and build. But his family's ways couldn't have been more different to mine.

The Beatties were great party-goers and party-givers. They lived in a big house on Duncairn Gardens, and in their drawing room Herbie and his three attractive sisters could pound the piano or render a song as naturally as breathing. I always thought they were a lovely family.

It was to be a proper party, no doubt about that. Herbie's mother was to preside, and his sisters would be there. All guests were obviously going to be in full party fig. Invitations had been issued to selected boys and girls, and there was none of your dirt about the chosen ones either. Nearly all came from the parlour house belt, and could be relied on to have some sort of rudimentary idea of the social graces: postman's knock, pass the parcel — that sort of thing. Also, no doubt, a game once described to me by Herbie where you kiss someone in the dark, then call out the name of the person you think it was. The lights go up, to reveal somebody hitching his trousers up, as if his bum's just been kissed. All these games I'd heard of, but I'd never played any of them, and me eleven too.

There had never been any parties run in our house in Cosgrave Street for the simple reason that there wasn't any room in it. If you opened the front door and took a longish step you were on the edge of the hearth. The only parties I'd ever been to were the ones run in Newington Church and I didn't even belong to it. I'll tell you better than that — I wasn't even invited to the two parties in Newington Church that I had attended. At the first one Fat Campbell and I let on our tickets had been pinched out of our pockets in the milling crowd trying to get in the door of the church hall, bursting into tears and successfully melting the heart of the lady collecting the tickets. On the second occasion the two of us actually did the pocket-picking; then from inside the doorway we successfully pleaded for our victims to be admitted to the party, as they stood there roaring and crying at the door.

And now Herbie Beattie had invited me most warmly to his party. It made me quite nervous.

When the time came to get ready it suddenly dawned on Mother and me that I had no shoes. Nothing except mutton dummies. And at that, they were busted. They were all gaping and grinning at the toes.

It was all right to wear a passable jacket and trousers, both made up by a wee woman in Lawther Place from a suit of our Jack's. It was even all right

17

to wear a shirt of .Tommy's that had a line of stitching up the back of the collar to make it fit my pipestem of a neck. All that was dead-on. But — finishing it off with busted mutton-dummies?

'I'll whiten them up for you, son,' Mother said, encouragingly, 'it'll make them like new.' She applied whitening with loving care. She even touched up the inside of the piece at each toe, where it curled up and out. Then she dried them in front of the fire.

'I don't think anybody ever wears mutton-dummies to a party with their good suit,' I said, doubtfully, 'not even good mutton-dummies.'

'Go on ahead, darlin'' Mother said, 'you're just lovely lookin'.' She ushered me to the door, gave me the usual kiss, and watched me walk up Cosgrave Street to the party.

I wasn't three minutes out of the house when the rain came belting down. Before I was even halfway to Herbie Beattie's I had left the whitening from my slippers behind in a hundred streaks on the pavement. My socks were sodden, and my feet were squelching under me.

In the doorway of a shop almost opposite Herbie Beattie's house I took up my position. Standing well in from the swirls of rain I saw that the lights were bright in the drawing room; figures were moving about. Hardly conscious of the passage of time I watched the arrival of each guest. Herbie's mother met each one at the door. She seemed to be wearing a sort of flowery gown. Once I saw her cigarette glow in the night.

Watching in the darkness I saw the front door open once, and Herbie come out. He stood looking

Harry McQuillan of Dunluce

must have been about ten before I discovered that
 didn't actually have relatives called McQuillan
 ving in Dunluce Castle on the North Antrim coast.
 ndeed I didn't even know that Dunluce Castle was
 ruin until about the same time. It took my mother
 o mention it one night after she got back from a
 Mother's Union outing to Portrush.

It was a great disappointment to me. My Uncle
 Harry McQuillan certainly hadn't said anything
 bout ruins.

'My family's related to the McQuillans of
 Dunluce Castle, you know,' he would announce in
 is fine clear voice, and upstairs in bed our Jim and
 Tommy and Charlotte and me, we could hear him
 uite distinctly over the hubbub of my father's first
 ight home from sea.

My Uncle Harry McQuillan was a moderate man,
 ut he always broke out for that first night of
 ather's home coming. It was expected of him. In
 act, to tell you the truth he was summoned to the
 resence. Myself or our Tommy or Charlotte or Jim
 ould be sent round to Uncle Harry McQuillan's
 use in Meadow Street in North Belfast. It would
 ve been round about the seven o'clock mark on

22

In the doorway of a shop I took up my position.

19

up and down the road for a bit, then he went back inside again. Looking for me, I thought.

Every quarter of an hour or so an almost-empty tram ground its way either up or down the track. The drivers were buttoned up snugly against the cold. I could hear the piano playing, and snatches of song.

Once the light in the drawing room went out. I know what that means, I thought, putting the heel of one foot on to the toe of another, to squeeze the water out. As the light went on again, to the accompaniment of squeals and screams, I nodded to myself. Yes, it was the trouser trick all right.

The night wore on. There was more singing and music in Herbie's house, then there was a quiet spell. They're eating, I said, I'll bet you anything you like they're eating. Sausage rolls and that. Probably fancy sandwiches and buns and things.

Now it was quite late. The rain had stopped and a wan and washed out moon tried to peep through the clouds. Suddenly Herbie Beattie's front door opened and two girls, dressed for the road, came out. 'Good night, girls,' Mrs Beattie called, and Herbie, behind her in the doorway echoed 'Cheerio.' The girls, murmuring contentedly together, walked up Duncairn Gardens with linked arms.

The party was breaking up. I left the dark doorway, broke into a run to warm myself up, and to ease the stiffness, and made my way back home.

Mother was waiting up. 'Was the party nice?' she wanted to know.

'Sticking out,' I said. 'It was great.' I kicked off the sodden slippers, peeled the wet socks away from

my feet, and wriggled my toes in front of

'You look awful cold, son,' Mother sai at my blue knees with concern.

'It's all right,' I told her, 'I'm getting

'Would you like something to eat? asked, still looking at me closely. 'Th morrow's broth there. It'll warm you up.'

I looked at her in astonishment. ' laughed at the very idea. 'Broth? Afte Herbie Beattie's parties? After sausage buns and stuff!' I looked at Mother as if s all in it or something.

'That's nice,' Mother said, and bent ov me good night. Then she picked up her water bottle from beside the hob, and pull up by the steep banister rail to bed.

my feet, and wriggled my toes in front of the fire.

'You look awful cold, son,' Mother said, looking at my blue knees with concern.

'It's all right,' I told her, 'I'm getting warm.'

'Would you like something to eat?' Mother asked, still looking at me closely. 'There's to-morrow's broth there. It'll warm you up.'

I looked at her in astonishment. 'Broth?' I laughed at the very idea. 'Broth? After one of Herbie Beattie's parties? After sausage rolls and buns and stuff!' I looked at Mother as if she wasn't all in it or something.

'That's nice,' Mother said, and bent over to kiss me good night. Then she picked up her stone hot water bottle from beside the hob, and pulled herself up by the steep banister rail to bed.

Harry McQuillan of Dunluce

I must have been about ten before I discovered that I didn't actually have relatives called McQuillan living in Dunluce Castle on the North Antrim coast. Indeed I didn't even know that Dunluce Castle was a ruin until about the same time. It took my mother to mention it one night after she got back from a Mother's Union outing to Portrush.

It was a great disappointment to me. My Uncle Harry McQuillan certainly hadn't said anything about ruins.

'My family's related to the McQuillans of Dunluce Castle, you know,' he would announce in his fine clear voice, and upstairs in bed our Jim and Tommy and Charlotte and me, we could hear him quite distinctly over the hubbub of my father's first night home from sea.

My Uncle Harry McQuillan was a moderate man, but he always broke out for that first night of Father's home coming. It was expected of him. In fact, to tell you the truth he was summoned to the presence. Myself or our Tommy or Charlotte or Jim would be sent round to Uncle Harry McQuillan's house in Meadow Street in North Belfast. It would have been round about the seven o'clock mark on

miss out on the hard bit. But our Tommy and Jim and Charlotte and me, we were in a state of silent panic till the performance was over.

All these memories came back to me when I took a run out to see Dunluce Castle at the end of last Spring. Seeing its lovely ruins against the sea and the evening sky, I could hear again as clearly as if it was only last night the sound of the singing and laughing coming up the stairs, when I was a wee boy whose Daddy was home from the sea.

And I couldn't help thinking it's a pity Dunluce is a ruin. If it had been a real castle, it would have been lovely to go up and hammer on the front door, and say, the way I did half a century ago: 'Is my Uncle Harry McQuillan in?'

Mart and the Flute

I can still remember as if it was yesterday the sight of our Mart sitting in front of the fire in our kitchen, his feet up on the hob, playing sad tunes on the flute, with the tears blinding him.

This is a proper flute I'm talking about, mind you — not one of these tin whistles. Mart was trying very hard to reach the standard for Lilliview Flute Band, and he was practising like the devil. He was about sixteen at this time, so that would make it 1929. Lilliview Flute Band was having a good year, so they had a waiting list for fluters.

With seven people in a wee small kitchen house Mart came in for some right bantering, as you can imagine. But he never mismade himself, he just tootled away there, with the tears running down his face half the time.

It's funny, that, isn't it? I must say I've never heard of any other fluter crying when he was playing the sentimental stuff. It's a good thing James Galway's not afflicted with the same complaint, because he has to stand right out where everybody can see him, when he's at the fluting. It wouldn't half put a dampener on his concerts if he had to knock off in the middle of Mozart, the way our Mart

*He just tootled away there, with tears running
down his face.*

had to do, in order to blow his nose.

Mart didn't seem to be able to help himself, though. He didn't sob, mind you, or anything like that. It was just that he turned on the waterworks once he got into Londonderry Air territory.

'Maybe you'd be as well to stick to "The Sash My Father Wore",' some of the brothers told him once, 'for so help my God some of these days that flute's going to turn to liquorice in your hands, with the action of the water on the wood.'

'I can't help it,' Mart said moistly, and went back to 'Smiling Through'.

Well, actually, he never did reach the standard for Lilliview Flute Band, but there was certainly once when he had the satisfaction of appearing in public with the band, as they say, live. That was when young Joe Mercer went away to the States.

Joe was fourteen: one of a family of five. He had an uncle in Brooklyn — as who hadn't? This uncle owned a shop where Joe was to work. Actually, the way Joe told us about it was that his uncle owned a store: you know the way the Americans call a shop a store? Well since the only store I knew was a pork store, I remember thinking Joe was going to work in a long, narrow place with whitewashed walls and a long, white-tiled counter, and sides of bacon hanging all over the place. The sort of place where kids like myself walked in and asked for tuppence worth of griskins for the dinner.

Anyway, there was a bit of an atmosphere building up when the time came for Joe Mercer's departure. It was quite an event in our part of Tiger's Bay. The women of Cosgrave Street were running in and slipping him a threepenny bit and a wee hug.

Or if they hadn't the money, just giving him a wee hug on its own. He was going away by himself after all.

You could nearly always tell when something special was going to happen in our street. There was a kind of tingle about, you know? Well, wearing up to Joe leaving you would have thought there was an electric current running up and down the street: definitely something was on.

Out came Joe to the front door, with his wee suitcase and brown paper parcel, and Mrs Mercer crying sore. He gave her and his two sisters an embarrassed hug and a kiss, and he set off with his da and his brother down Cosgrave Street, only to be stopped by somebody's outstretched hand about twenty yards from his own house.

This fellow held out his hand like a points peeler, and stopped Joe and his party at the junction with Lilliput Street. The next thing what do you think but up struck the rolls of the side drums and bass drum and out from Lilliput Street marched Lilliview Flute Band. They fell in behind Joe Mercer and his party in the middle of the street and away they went great stuff down Cosgrave Street. I'm telling you the crashing of the drums and the swing of the music was something to talk about, marching Joe Mercer to the States.

Talk about a send-off! Joe Mercer's mother was as proud as anything that night.

And who's in the back row of the fluters, twiddling his fingers with the best of them, with his head to the side, letting on to read the music that was strapped to his wrist? Right. Our Mart — he'd made it at last. His first and only public appearance.

Being only a wee fellow I wasn't allowed to go down to the Liverpool boat with them. But I know they gave the passengers a grand selection at the quayside that night. And when Joe Mercer was leaning over the side of the boat listening to the sad Irish airs I'll bet you anything you like he never noticed the fluter who was paying him the biggest compliment of them all.

For although Lilliview Flute Band were all desperate sorry to see Joe Mercer going away to America, it's the City Hall to a toasted crumpet our Mart was the only one there in the band who was actually crying about it.

The Good Blue Suit

My father kept his shore-going navy blue suit hanging up in the wardrobe in our front room. It was a fine tailored suit and it carried his smell of tobacco and John Jamieson whiskey in every fibre. One day when my mother was well out of the road in my Aunt Lena's house in Ardoyne, and my father was even further away in Galveston, Texas, on board the *Dunaff Head*, my younger brother Jim and I searched the pockets of the good blue suit.

The first thing we found was a foreign-looking packet with two cheroots in it. Although Jim and I were only twelve and fourteen we had been seasoned smokers for some time, so we grabbed the cheroots with some eagerness, as being a big improvement on the butts that our Jack, who was allowed to smoke, left in the ashtray beside his bed.

So help my good God, I'll never forget the first pull at that cheroot. I thought I was sent for. It was like drawing in a lungful of the smoke that comes out of those sulphur candles — you know, the ones you use to kill bugs in the house. Our Jim and me, we nearly had an attack of the bends, 'gasping for breath up in our front room. It didn't half put my father up a notch or two in my estimation. He must have had lungs like leather. I suppose it was working in amongst all the oil fumes in the engine room that did it.

The pockets of his suit always carried a few foreign coins as well. We found American and Canadian coins, and Dutch and German money as well, in all the wee hidden pockets that suits had in those days. There was one time when our Jim was sixteen he got a tip for a dog and he paid his way into the cheap side of the dog track with a Canadian ten cent piece he knocked off out of my father's shore-going suit. He didn't want to break into the stake of two shillings that he was keeping for backing the tip, you see.

Since this happened forty years ago I don't suppose the dog track'll take any action on this information, even though I have named names. In any case the dog was hammered.

'It ate its bed,' explained the fellow who gave our Jim the tip. If our Jim had been allowed anywhere near that dog it wouldn't have eaten another bed for a brave while, I'll tell you that much.

I'll tell you another thing too: if my father had ever found out that our Jim had hit the turnstile with a Canadian dime it would have been very awkward for a bit. My father might have been a small man but he was very much the head of the house. He was never really absent, you see. My mother was continually making reference to him in her conversation. As long as ever I can remember she was head over heels in love with him. Even though she'd had ten kids by him she still got into a state of excitement when he arrived home at the front door with his white seaman's bag over his shoulder, after months away at sea.

A couple or three hours after his arrival the two of them would head away down Cosgrave Street, making for the town, with their arms linked, and my father wearing his good blue suit. It was lovely to see them. We kids used to be all delighted watching them going off down the town like that. Even if my father hadn't bunged each one of us sixpence it would have been nice to see them anyway.

Do you know this? Every single letter that my father wrote to my mother — and he was a great letter-writer — started off 'My Darling Lizzie' and ended up 'Your own Marriott' — that was his name: Marriott — and there must have been about thirty kisses in neat rows at the foot of each letter. We used to read them, me and our Jim, when my mother was out.

That trip down the town on the day the *Dunaff Head* arrived back in Belfast was a custom of many years in our family. Actually, if she'd told the truth I don't think my mother was all that keen on the custom, for what happened was my father blew in pounds and pounds of his pay-off money on pieces of extravagant nonsense. Long before there was such a thing as a washing machine in Tiger's Bay my father landed one home from one of these trips to town. It was a big brute of a thing that was worked by pushing and shoving a handle back and forwards, thereby stirring the clothes about inside the machine. Our Jim and me we got the job of operating it more often than any of the rest of the family, and there were times when we could have seen the old man far enough. Long before it was worn out my mother gave the washing machine to Bennett, the ragman, for half a dozen cups and saucers.

Another time my father and mother landed home with a record player as big as a tea chest. It could handle ten records at once, another first for Tiger's Bay. When these contraptions were presented to her my mother used to put a brave face on, but I'm sure she could have found a better use for the money.

Still, when my father was away, she brushed his good shore-going suit regularly. It sort of represented my father during his absence at sea.

That suit had an authority all of its own. And just to emphasise its position in our house I can tell you this: it never saw the inside of a pawnshop in its life.

Sea Fever

When I was a young fellow of fourteen or fifteen they didn't have any of those books that told parents how to bring up kids. Even if there had been, my mother wouldn't have bothered reading them — she was too busy having kids and rearing them to read books.

Well, as a result of having no advisory literature to keep her right in the matter my mother used to tell us kids lies every now and again, not knowing the desperate, dire consequences of such a thing on young minds. Against that of course we youngsters didn't know that our minds were supposed to be susceptible to things like that. So there was no harm done. It was cancelled out.

One of the lies that my mother told me when I was fourteen was that it would be all right for me to go to sea some time in a Head Line ship, like my father. My old dad joined in the deception too when he came home every lot of months.

I should have guessed, all the same, that there wasn't a big lot of weight behind their promises. If I'd only thought about it carefully enough I'd have noticed that whenever I raised the subject of going away to sea both my mother and father used to say

'Mmm Hmm'. Anybody who knows Belfast people could tell you right away that 'Mmm Hmm' means nothing, and that applies today just as much as it did forty years ago.

But I heard what I wanted to hear whenever I asked about going to sea. So long as the answer wasn't no I was carried away in my imagination, up to the eyes in flung spray and blown spume, hanging on for dear life out there on the jib boom doing whatever it was that the old time sailors did on jib booms.

During the early 1930s I hung around the Belfast docks every single chance I could get. I was daft about ships. Luckily, deck officers in those days were very understanding with wee boys who had sea fever. I asked many a crusty-looking officer of the watch if I could go on board and it wasn't very often I was refused.

I went up the gangway of the *Torr Head* when I was only thirteen and told the Chief Officer the tale about my father being the donkeyman of the *Dunaff Head*, and about my own ambition to be a sailor. He wrote me out a note on Head Line paper that said 'To whom it may concern: Sam McAughtry would like a job at sea and I can recommend him.' He signed it and handed it to me: 'There you are now,' he said, 'keep that till you're sixteen and it might get you a job.'

'If you ever want your bicycle fixed cheap,' I told him in gratitude, 'there's a man three doors below us'll do it for you. He can make dog kennels too,' I said, to show him the range of my influence.

'Thanks very much all the same,' said the Chief Officer of the *Torr Head*, 'but ships' carpenters

Deck officers in those days were very understanding with wee boys who had sea fever.

37

actually seem to do nothing else but make dog kennels for their friends the whole time they're at sea. So it's all right, thanks.'

With my old school mate Herbie Beattie I even went on board the little, immaculately maintained ship that carried Belfast's sewage into the Irish Sea and dumped it there. Any kind or make of a ship did me, so long as it went through salt water. I walked around ancient British-built steamships sold to the Greeks, marvelling at the farmyard smell about them, and the crated pigs and poultry on their decks.

I was on board the famous four-masted barque *Herzogin Cecilie* when she called into Belfast in the course of the Australian grain trade. That was a ship to stir a young fellow's blood. The *Herzogin Cecilie* had nothing more romantic in her holds than paving stones for ballast when I was on board, but I looked down there and saw Spanish gold and jewels. And although she had bare yards and was moored up against a very modern concrete grain silo I stood on her deck, braced myself against the tilt of her, and heard the banshee moaning of the wind through her shrouds, and don't try to tell me that I didn't.

When the *Dunaff Head*, my father's ship, tied up in Belfast I was always the second one on board — straight after the customs man. Down to the fo'c'sle I went, to be handed immediately a huge chunk of ship's cake and a mug of sweet tea by the nearest seaman. It's no wonder I used to say to my mother every now and again, 'I hope my daddy's getting that job fixed up for me in the Head Line.'

'Mmm Hmm,' she would say and it was only

when I was fifteen that I discovered that 'Mmm Hmm' meant I was too good at my books to go to sea. They had a white collar job in mind for me.

'Seafaring's a rough dirty life son,' my mother used to say to me apologetically, after I'd started the white collar job.

Those were the days when kids were never openly critical of their mothers and fathers. So whenever my mother used to tell me that seafaring wasn't the life for me, I just used to look at her and say 'Mmm Hmm'.

Come on Kaye Don!

As far as the Germans were concerned our forgiveness came more slowly after the First War than after the Second.

In 1928, ten years after the Armistice, the rounded part of a slice of plain loaf was known in our family as the German side, and the straight-edged slice was called the British side. We used to complain bitterly at the table when Mother made us take German sides.

It follows, therefore, that we Tiger's Bay kids fully accepted the reports circulating in Belfast that the German drivers in the Tourist Trophy race carried long knives so that they could reach over at high speed and slash the tyres of such Bulldog Drummond figures as Kaye Don, Captain Malcolm Campbell and Earl Howe.

I make it about 1930 when, together with a couple more nine-year-olds from our street, I decided to go along to the Ards circuit and see what all the talk was about.

Make no mistake, there *was* plenty of talk about it. The TT race had every bit as big a grip on the Ulster people fifty years ago as the 1978 World Cup had on the Argentinians. We lived and breathed and dreamt motor racing: on the big day the people of Ulster felt themselves to be at the centre of the universe.

So, after telling our mothers a pack of lies to make them think we were being looked after by big fellas we set off, the three of us, at half eight in the morning, to make our way to Dundonald.

Tracing the source of the Nile may have had more administrative problems than our journey, but it was no more intrepid. We hadn't the least idea where Dundonald was when we started.

Scotchy Graham's big brother saw us bouncing hopefully along York Street carrying our lemonade bottles and pieces. He pulled up in his laundry cart and invited us to jump aboard. Talk about sticking out — he was going to the TT race!

The pony clip-clopped up the unfamiliar Newtownards Road, and Butler Forsythe and Frankie Pattison and me, we stood up in the Laundry cart and shouted 'Come On Kaye Don.' He was our man, Kaye Don, in his Alfa Romeo and his white overalls.

We left Scotchy Graham's big brother somewhere not too far from where Stormont is now, for I remember a walk of about fifteen minutes to the Hairpin Bend. Thousands and thousands seemed to be there, all in great good humour. Everybody knew something exclusive about the drivers: names were being dropped, like Cyril Paul and Birkin and Caracciola.

'Nuvolari might win it,' somebody said.

'De Valera's in this race,' I told Butler Forsythe. 'I hope he doesn't win it,' we all said. We weren't Tiger's Bay boys for nothing.

The German's been disqualified! Everybody was talking about it — something to do with his super-charger. Leave it to the blinking Germans, they all said, you couldn't watch them. Of course, Earl Howe drove one of their Mercedes, but we didn't count him.

A bellowing stampede to the Hairpin Bend, whines and snarls and deep coughs, and there was the most exciting smell left behind the vanishing cars. It was a rich smell, the essence of speed and danger: the smell of ten thousand blowlamps. This was the TT race all right. But I couldn't properly see the cars.

The crowd cheered the thundering Bentleys and the prissy little Austins, two goggled and helmeted heads sitting up in each car. The rain came and I was soaked. Running towards a hedge for shelter I discovered that cows had been using my field, and I left a mutton dummy embedded in the proof. No matter, there was nobody here to tell me off. I sat in the pouring rain and had my piece and the last of the lemonade.

Messages were still going from mouth to mouth: Kaye Don's crashed, but he's OK. Birkin's crashed too, it must be the heavy rain. After a bit I could see the race fine — maybe I'll see a couple of skids. But no: to tell the truth it was a bit boring now. No tyres getting slashed: no nothing, but these cars whaling round and round.

Half four and it's all over. The Italian won it, everybody said. I was quite disappointed when I heard the name. Where was Malcolm Campbell, for dear's sake? What happened to Frazer-Nash?

Time for home in the pouring rain. No Butler

Forsythe and no Frankie. Not only that but no Scotchy Graham's big brother with his pony and cart. Ah well, time for the proven formula:

'Mister, I'm lost...'

'Where d'ye live, son?'

'Away in Cosgrave Street, Mister...'

'Here's tuppence. Jump on any one of them trams.'

The conductor comes up: 'I'm lost, Mister...' He gives me a weary look, passes by. Tuppence up on the day. Sticking out!

Six o'clock and into the house.

'My God, what's happened to you!' Mother yells, and before I can answer she fills a bucket of water and shoves it on the stove.

That's all she ever thinks of, I say to myself in disgust, washing people.

'Who won the race?' they're all asking me.

'De Valera,' I told them, 'isn't it desperate?'

The Good Life Reaches Tiger's Bay

I think I can pinpoint the time when hire purchase was imported into North Belfast from the USA. I would make it about 1931.

It actually started with wirelesses. Up until then maybe one house in thirty in Tiger's Bay would have had a wireless, worked through a cat's whisker and earphones. I remember the first time I put the earphones on and listened to a brass band — I genuinely thought it was the Salvation Army band from the York Street citadel. Matt Collins, the old fellow who owned the wireless nearly took his end laughing when I told him the Salvation Army was coming through the earphones.

The hire purchase wireless sets seemed to mushroom nearly overnight. One day Tiger's Bay was peaceful, its silence broken only by the sound of horses' hooves and iron wheels on the cobblestones; a fishmonger shouting 'Fresh herrin's alive'; the singing of children in their street games, or the screams of a housewife being chased into the street by her husband — ordinary things like that. Then, as if in a matter of hours, the whole neighbourhood was full of wireless sets in lovely plastic cases: you wouldn't believe it.

The whole neighbourhood was full of wireless sets in lovely plastic cases.

In the shops down along York Street there were all sorts of fancy notices in the windows. 'Half a Crown Down and Five Shillings a Week!' they said. 'Pay the Easy Way!' Oh, it was the American way of life all right, arriving in Tiger's Bay in style.

Everywhere you went, all up and down Cosgrave Street, round Mackey Street and Collyer Street and in and out of the whole Bay all you could hear was wireless sets belting away there, at maximum volume. It was enough to nearly deave you. I can't exactly compare it to music while you work because most of the men were out of work, but it was certainly a matter of music while you play banker, or pitch and toss.

Now there's no point in trying to make out that the people round our way could afford to pay five shillings a week for something on the hire purchase. For goodness sake the rent of a house wasn't even five shillings and yet there was big numbers of the neighbours couldn't even keep their rent books clear.

In any case, what money was left over from the rent and grub and the wee credit drapery man with the bad feet, was collared by the man of the house for a few pints.

No, there was no Klondyke waiting for the finance companies in Tiger's Bay. What there actually was, was a lot of women who couldn't believe their ears when they heard that all they had to do to get a brand new wireless in a plastic case was to get their men to sign a piece of paper and pay half a crown, and there they were, as good as the next one, with their own wireless sets.

Have you ever noticed the way some people nowadays like to keep their curtains pulled back in the evening time, and let the passers-by see all their nice furniture, and their colour television, and maybe their illuminated fish tank? They're proud of all their bits of things, you see, and there's nothing wrong with that. Well, it was the same sort of thing in Tiger's Bay whenever they all got their wireless sets. Naturally enough they couldn't put them on display, the way you do with an illuminated fish tank. There actually wasn't much point in rolling up the blind and letting people see right into your kitchen on account of the wireless even though, mind you, they looked nice and shiny, and some of them were done up to look the same as clocks, and the like of that. No, what the passers-by were more likely to see was the butter boxes being used instead of chairs.

So what they all did was to throw the front door open, do the same with the kitchen door, and turn up the volume like anything.

I'm telling you it didn't half make a difference to Tiger's Bay. Talk about music! When we weren't giving John McCormack a bit of a hand out in the garden where the praties grow, we were whistling Sousa marches, or else we were wishing whoever was playing Wagner would shut up.

It's no exaggeration to say those wireless sets were the best thing that had happened to the people of Tiger's Bay since the Armistice. They were the most exciting things they had ever owned.

Only of course they didn't own them. For they'd only paid the half crown down, and no instalments after that.

So the finance companies took them all away

47

again. House by house they had to give them back, and Tiger's Bay quietened down once more.

In time, of course, second hand wirelesses came on the market and gradually all the excitement went out of owning one. It was a good while before Tiger's Bay knew that fine, carefree feeling of prosperity again.

But sure we had a great time while it lasted. I'm telling you we certainly enjoyed the American way of life the first time it came round our way, and if the tick men did get a bit of a gunk out of it, well, that made it all the better.

Whatever Happened to Banker?

When I was a young lad in Tiger's Bay in Belfast before the war there was a terrible lot of banker played out in the streets. It's funny, but you never seem to hear of banker nowadays.

I suppose everybody knows the rules of the game: dear knows they're simple. One man holds the deck — he's the banker. Your hand's just a pile of cards face-downwards, and you back the card that shows when you turn it up, against the banker's hand. If your hand is the same value as the banker's, or less, you lose, and if the banker turns up an ace everybody loses. An ace is a clear board, we used to say.

Now why did we play banker out in the streets and up the entries? Why did we not play poker or something? I've thought about this. One good point in favour of banker was this: if the peeler interrupted your game it was a simple matter to grab the money off your own hand and get offside.

With poker, now, a raid by the peelers would have meant everybody in the school grabbing some of the pot before making off. And you know what that would have started. There would have been heads split. Everybody arguing about how much they had in the middle.

So to that extent anyway banker was probably an evolutionary game. Peelers like Fairy Feet, one of our local policemen, made it necessary. Fairy Feet could have materialised out of thin air, and mind you that's saying something when you remember I'm talking about the Belfast policemen of 1933. Each of them was a one man tug of war team.

Every time a banker school was set up a dicker out was appointed to stand watch. His job was to dick out for signs of the law, but Fairy Feet had a hundred tricks to beat the dicker out. One of his favourite ones was to tippy toe up an entry parallel to the street where the banker was going on, knock one of the entry doors and then go right through some woman's house and burst out of her front door right on top of the banker school. Talk about scattering!

In the days of the big depression — the Twenties and Thirties — the men of Tiger's Bay used to stand round the street corners in droves. Every day there was sure to be a banker school going on.

And nearby you'd have found us kids with our own card school following the same rules and rituals. We even set the cards out for mugs the way some of the men did, wetting the wee finger and using it to whip the bottom card away, after showing it to the mug and letting him think it was dealt out.

There was a considerable rigmarole in choosing which hand you were going to put your money on. This was done by tossing up for it. What we called weeking. When you were choosing between two hands you called one head and the other harp, and then you tossed up your lucky weeking halfpenny that was used for nothing else.

''Ead-'arp,' we would say, indicating the two hands we were arbitrating on. We never sounded the H's. ''Ead-'arp,' we said. Just like that.

Weeking was an extremely serious business, I'll tell you that. One or two people in the Bay actually held privileged positions on account of their weeking ability. These were the ones that were expected to make the decision, in a big banker school, as to which of the final two hands remaining was to be left to the banker.

Every eye was fixed on the weeker as he flicked the halfpenny into the air. He would already have said his 'ead-'arps and we would have said them with him. Up went the halfpenny and when it landed, it landed with a brave smack because the weeker brought his catching hand right up from the ground to meet it and the louder the smack the more certain it was that the banker was a doomed man.

I saw some right banker schools in those days. Schools so big they had three dicker outs, one at each end of the street and one on top of the yard wall to prevent Fairy Feet from doing his wee trick and coming out of a front door.

Mind you, the dicker out that was up on the yard wall had a chancy enough job. Well, it stands to sense if you're on a yard wall you can see people going to the yard can't you? I can tell you there's many a dicker out got a basin of water slung round him from some touchy housewife who wanted to go to the yard without doing it in front of an audience.

There were some heroic wins at the banker too. Like the day Banty Jackson lost his stick round to

Big Leachy and Happy Matchett.

They were in partnership this time, Big Leachy and Happy. Banty Jackson stopped his pony and cart full of firewood and watched the school out of curiosity. Then he started to nibble. Little did he know he had run into two men who had already cleaned up two lots of unemployment benefit plus the funds of a pigeon club.

Within fifteen minutes Banty had lost his stick round. When the game was over Big Leachy and Happy Matchett drove off to McEldowney's pub sitting on Banty Jackson's cart full of sticks and poor Banty was left standing there stunned.

You would never see things like that nowadays, all the same, would you?

I bet you there's none of these young ones now could week between two hands the way we could, down round Tiger's Bay.

Anyway, there's none of them now that can play banker. If I thought there was anybody wanted to learn it I wouldn't mind wetting the wee finger and showing them a thing or two.

Son of a Donkeyman

Cosgrave Street in Belfast, where I was born, looked right down on to York Dock where the Head Line deep sea freighters tied up. My father was donkeyman on one of these ships, the *Dunaff Head*. When she was in port her upper works and her black funnel with its Red Hand of Ulster could be seen clearly from all the wee streets that made up Sailortown and Tiger's Bay.

As a young kid I used to be wildly excited when my father came home. The other ones in the street used to pull my leg. 'So the donkeyman's home again,' they would say.

In case you don't know it, the donkeyman on the old steamships was boss over the trimmers and firemen and greasers. He was the leading hand in the engine room: a petty officer. His bosses were the engineers. He was the only engine room rating in the Head Line with his own cabin.

So, in our family we were very proud of the fact that my old dad was a donkeyman. My father had reached the top in his job. When I was a youngster I expected everybody to recognise this. When they didn't and when the other kids joked about it, I was flabbergasted.

Here's the way the hierarchy went. You had the trimmer right at the bottom. He was all alone in the dark bunker, trimming and levelling the coal and wheeling it in a barrow over to the chutes where he emptied it down to where the firemen were working in the stokehold. What with the deck heaving and pitching all the time it couldn't have been any kind of a cakewalk, trimming in the Head Line ships on the North Atlantic run.

Then you had the fireman, the next step up. There were two firemen to cover nine fires: they did five and four each by turns.

Nearly everybody knows what a fireman did, using the shovel to fire the boilers, but not many people know that, while he was sweating like a pig, he was liable to be suddenly drenched in freezing cold water, due to the waves crashing in through the fiddley, or the ventilators. It couldn't have been good for them could it?

The next promotion was a welcome one, for it got the fireman out of the stokehold and into the engine room as a greaser. He did practically nothing but squeeze oil out of a long can into the moving parts, feeling them with the other hand to see if they were overheating. Forty minutes to do the whole lot and then start all over again. There was one greaser and one engineer on watch on the engine room together.

For a few bob extra a week the greaser might move up to storekeeper. He was still oiling the engines, but he kept a tally on all the tools and paintbrushes and so on that were handed out. And then right at the top was the donkeyman greaser, in charge of all those people I mentioned, although

Into our tiny wee house he would land the bo'sun, the lamptrimmer and the ship's carpenter.

mind you he never actually bothered much with them, for they all knew what they were doing.

The donkeyman got his name because, as well as being a greaser at sea, he fired the one boiler that kept the wee donkey engine going on deck when cargo was being worked in port. He got a bit of overtime money for that.

Now, being a senior man in the crew, my father tended to drink with the other senior men when he was ashore. Into our wee tiny house in Cosgrave Street some nights he would land the bo'sun, the lamptrimmer, and the ship's carpenter, and upstairs in bed we kids would hear them yarning and singing and clinking their glasses and complimenting my mother on her beauty.

On nights like this my father used to send my mother upstairs to fetch one of us kids down to meet the company. It was either our Jim or Tommy or me who was called. We would be lying in the darkness, waiting for the summons, each one of us practising the Ten Commandments, and helping each other with the hard ones, the ones about graven images, and the like of that.

'Sam,' Mother would whisper softly at the bedroom door. It was me! Sticking out!

Downstairs in the gaslight, blinking, loving the pipe smoke, drinking in every detail of the navy blue-suited seamen, their kindly faces smiling at me.

'Say the Ten Commandments, son,' Dad would say, one arm around my waist. When he was seated I reached his shoulder.

'The first commandment is...' I would begin, knowing that Jim and Tommy were out on the landing, silently giving me a hand.

'Very good, Donkey,' the bo'sun would say across to my father when all the ox-ing and assing was said correctly. 'Isn't he a smart kid, Lampy?' Dad would say to the lamptrimmer. Then all four of them would hand over a shilling each and deliver a whiskery, Guinnessy, lovely kiss. The four bob was handed to Mother, waiting at the turn of the stairs for it. She'd have been a mug if she didn't. We got a penny each from her in the morning, and that was plenty for our needs.

So there you are now. That's the sort of thing that happened to you when you were the son of a donkeyman. I always think my father left me a lovely legacy. Sooner or later when two or three are gathered together in a pub or some place the talk'll come round to what father did.

I just wait my turn. When the son of the tinker, and the son of the tailor have had their say, I give it a few seconds silence for effect, then: 'My father,' I say, with a smile of pure pride, 'my father was a donkeyman.'

The Inniskillings' War Pipes

Paul McCartney's hit record 'Mull of Kintyre' has come and gone, but I'll certainly remember it. I loved the way the Campbelltown Pipe Band eased into the melody after a nice long introduction by the other instruments. The blend of the pipes and other band instruments is really something special.

I first heard this combination one evening back in 1935, at the tattoo that used to be held annually in the arena at the Balmoral Showgrounds in Belfast. Standing just inside the fenced enclosure I waited for the high point of the evening — a demonstration of marching and music by the combined bands of the Inniskilling Fusiliers.

As long as I live I'll remember the first, distant notes of the Inniskillings' war pipes, as, still unseen, the band approached the entrance to the arena. The music from the keyed chanter of the Irish war pipes is peculiarly shrill and exciting. When the brilliant arc lamps picked out the leading pipers, and my eye took in the saffron kilts, the green shawls, and the distinctive Irishness of their low-set swagger, I was completely captivated.

They were playing 'Killaloe', a bouncy, insolent march, as they took possession of the green field.

As the sound grew and the regiment approached, I tell you I felt like rushing out there, and marching with them.

Right into the centre of the enclosure the pipers strode. I saw that a whole silver band marched behind the pipes, their instruments at the ready, the drummers with their sticks poised. The regimental band marched the full length of the field to the air of 'Killaloe', and the thousands watching were as motionless as I was. Then the soldiers counter-marched: as they approached again there was a three-pace roll of the drums; the musicians were slow marching, and, for the first time in my life I heard the unique sound of silver and pipes blending.

They were playing 'Eileen Alana', one of our family's favourite tunes. Of their whole marching and playing programme that rendering of 'Eileen Alana' is the memory that remains sharper than any other. When the saffron-kilted pipers finally swung proudly through the exit arch, and the desolate wail of the pipes faded and died, I stood there applauding wildly, almost crying with the excitement of it.

A few days later I turned up, a skinny malink, at the foot of Cosgrave Street in Tiger's Bay. Here in a loft at the end of a stable yard the pipers and drummers of Castleton Temperance Pipe Band (Founded 1900) practised their skills. It was a powerful far cry from the Inniskilling Fusiliers, but it was all I could manage.

'I want to learn the pipes,' I said to the pipe major. There were vacancies for pipers, so I was taken on. Within a month I was playing the full instrument.

The Scottish pipes were heavy in their demand for wind, especially for a lad of fourteen, so they stopped one of my three drones. In three months or so there I was, out on the street at the election of Hall-Thompson, a full piper with the Castleton Temperance Pipe Band (Founded 1900).

My father was home from the sea, and, with Mother, he came up to Carlisle Circus to see me march with the Junior Orangemen.

'Where did you get the Western Ocean roll?' Dad wanted to know when I got home that night.

'You look like a refugee from a jumble sale,' one of the brothers told me, when he first saw me in uniform. But I felt good in cocked hat, shawl, tunic, cross-belts, kilt, sporran and spats. It was a great feeling to be out there with the pipers playing tunes with names that opened up the whole world: 'The 79th's Farewell to Gibraltar' was one. 'From Kantara to El Arish' was another. I swaggered along Belfast streets playing 'The Burning Sands of Egypt' and in the loft of an evening I stood with the band and set Cosgrave Street jigging with the 'Irish Washerwoman'.

I marched on the Twelfth Day with the big Orangemen. It was hard going for a boy piper. Starting off in the morning the lips are hard and fixed tightly around the mouthpiece of the pipes. But reaching Tiger's Bay after maybe ten miles of marching, the lips are slack and almost useless, and the pipes are on the edge of caterwauling exhaustion. Afterwards the sound of the music battered away at my brain and stayed there until I fell asleep on the Twelfth night.

When I was seventeen I gave the pipes up, and I've rarely played them since.

I saw two more tattoos at Balmoral after that first one. The Inniskillings performed at both. Their spell on me was as firm as ever, even though I knew the tricks of piping by then. I stood just as rapt from entrance to exit, and cheered as wildly when the sweet sound of the pipes and silver died finally away.

There could never be a better sound than that. Nobody could ever lift me to the wonderful heights that the Inniskilling Fusiliers did on those soft summer evenings over forty years ago.

But even so — that Paul McCartney and the Campbelltown Pipe Band are very good too, you know...

Collecting Skins

Only a matter of weeks ago I ran into a very well-known political man in a downtown Belfast pub. I'd been wanting to see him for some considerable time in connection with a thing I'm writing, so, since we both had half an hour or so to spare, we stood up at the bar and talked.

Now I suppose anybody seeing us standing there, with this fellow so famous and everything, would have thought we were discussing momentous affairs of state, such as the forthcoming election to the European Parliament, or whether the pound was in for another dose of galloping consumption, or the like of that.

Well somebody overhearing us would have been slightly surprised. For here's what we were actually talking about:

'Tell me this,' I asked him, 'whenever you were a kid before the war did you ever collect skins?'

I should explain here that I was talking about swill, for pigs. Waste food, you know. We called it collecting skins because it was mostly made up of potato and turnip skins.

'Did I ever collect skins?' this household name replied, 'I didn't half!'

'How much did you get for them?' I wanted to know.

'Tuppence a bucket for raw skins, and threepence for boiled,' he told me.

'It just goes to show you,' I observed, 'inflation was at its work even then — forty odd years ago. You were operating at the skins about five years after my time, and in my day we only got a penny for raws and tuppence for boileds.'

'But of course,' says your man, 'over on your side of the New Lodge Road you had your pig keepers, and over on our side we had ours.'

That sounded factual enough to me. I nodded agreement. 'I mean to say,' he said, 'they might have been using different rates, never mind inflation.'

'A very valid point,' I said graciously.

'There was a fellow kept three big sows in a stable yard in North Queen Street,' my companion said, 'and so help my God you could hardly get into the place for flies. You had to fight your way past them.' He paused, reliving the experience. 'It was like that Alfred Hitchcock picture, "The Birds",' he finished, 'you really felt threatened.'

'One thing I remember,' I said, 'was the territorial disputes, regarding who was entitled to knock which back doors.' We then began to touch on the competitive aspect of collecting skins, in our wee corner of the city.

By this time we had an audience of six, standing round us at the bar, letting on to read their papers, or studying the lettuce in their sandwiches, but actually all hanging on like grim death to the words of this famous figure, and his unfamous companion.

'You could hardly get into the place for flies.'

The lady behind the bar, she wasn't doing any letting on at all — she was openly standing twelve inches away, eyeball to eyeball, with her face all lively, and nodding her head and laughing whenever we did.

'When I was about eleven,' I said, 'I was challenged by a wee fellow up an entry in Spamount Street — frontier terrain,' I reminded my companion. He nodded, understandingly. 'There was only the two of us,' I went on, 'approaching each other like gunfighters in the Wild West. Only of course you didn't get gunfighters approaching each other in the old days with a bucket of skins in each hand.'

The great man was enjoying the crack. Around us there was complete silence. I went on: 'There wasn't enough room in the entry for the two of us to get past each other. So we put our buckets down. "This is my entry," I said to this wee fellow, "clear off, son." "Oh, if that a fact?" he replies, and hits me a looter across the side of the ear. Well of course,' I told my audience, 'when you're only eleven a fight can last a week. The pair of us fought till we were bored, then we picked up our buckets, made room for each other to get past, and away we went, undefeated.'

I looked at my companion: 'Do you know who that other boy was?' I asked. 'No,' says he. 'No,' says the lady behind the bar, and, still letting on to look at their sandwiches, the other six shook their heads slowly.

'It was Terry McS,' I said, mentioning the name of a man who became a smashing welterweight boxer later on. 'So,' I said, 'whenever anybody asks me nowadays do I remember Terry McS, I always say 'Remember him? For goodness sake I fought a draw with him.'

After this famous Belfastman had stopped laughing, he finished his drink and looked at his watch: 'You'll have to excuse me,' he said, 'I have a television appointment.'

'Oh, that's all right,' I said, with one eye on the barmaid and the six sandwich watchers; 'sure I have a broadcasting engagement myself.'

Nicknames

You don't hear nicknames used very much nowadays, do you? Not even a quarter as much as in my young day.

Listen to a group of young fellows anywhere when they're relaxing. If you were on a pint for every nickname you heard you would still go home sober.

Right enough, the soccer men still use nicknames to some extent. The sports pages still carry names like Bumper Graham and Bimbo Weatherup. I daresay there's the odd Dinger Bell still kicking a ball about too, but even here they're thin on the ground, compared to the great pre-war names, like Boy Martin, and Soldier Jones, and special heroes along York Street in Belfast over sixty years ago, Shooter Flack, and Silver Gough of Crusaders.

When I was a nipper in the Twenties and Thirties we hung labels on nearly everybody. Not long ago I ran into Ducky Kelso, so-called after the white ducks he wore in the Navy.

'What about Cloot?' I asked him, meaning his left-handed brother.

'He's in the care of the doctor,' I was told, and the name of the doctor was mentioned.

'Would he be anything to Doctor Iodine?' I

wanted to know, thinking of a famous practitioner in Belfast, who prescribed iodine for everything, including fractures. It turned out he was a son.

I learned that Hooky Millar was dead of the goitre, and Heelball had been crippled by a hundredweight of Arran Banners that had popped one of his discs out at the docks. Heelball, who used to be a shoemaker, got his name from the black stuff that made the edge of the heels nice and shiny. Between the two of us we ranged over a good many biographies: Bendy Shaw, Gunner Gordon, and old Golden Guts — he was supposed to have swallowed a gold sovereign once. They said his wife trailed him everywhere he went, for the hours immediately after his experience.

When these modern young fellows meet up again in another thirty odd years' time, their conversation'll be desperate grey, and plain:

'Whatever happened to Duncan?'

'Oh, he went into business with Ashley.'

'Really? And what about his chum Andrew?'

'Why, didn't you know? He and Cedric have been students at the Polytech for the last thirty years. They're studying social science.'

I think the woman's influence has a big lot to do with it. They're dead struck on these fancy names, like Jeremy for example. Jeremy acts on the TV, or else he's a character from the pages of some women's magazine. The fond mother in a parlour house in East Belfast who has named her son Jeremy would claw your eyes out if you tried to tell her that his real name's Jeremiah, and that Jeremy's only a nickname that's stuck fast.

Mothers in my time not only didn't mind nick-

Golden Guts

names being pinned on to their sons, they actually used the same titles themselves:

'Is Rattler in?' I used to ask one of our neighbours, when I wanted to play with her son.

'Rattler!' she would yell up the stairs, 'you're a-wantin.'

I can just picture the outrage of some of these semi-detached madames nowadays, if a wee boy knocked their door calling their son Rattler. He would get a looter in the eye with a tin of *pâte de fois gras*, so he would.

One of the memories that sticks very tightly in my mind is of mitching school one glorious summer's day with Blow Kennedy, so-called because he was the biggest liar in the County Antrim, and Happy Matchett. They were mates in a different school of mine and their teacher was a much-feared man known as Horsey McMullan. We began by climbing the wall into old Cornhat McClean's yard in Cosgrave Street, hunting rats in the stables. We were chased out by Porterbelly, one of Cornhat's drivers. Then we went up to the waterworks pond, to torment One-Wing, the park ranger in charge. One Wing'd lost an arm in the Boer War.

Then we went home and had our dinners. After that we headed down to the railway station in York Street, to see if we could earn a few coppers carrying bags for passengers, only to find that Bucksy Jamieson's gang had taken the station over for that very purpose. We had to run for our lives. At my suggestion we went down to the docks and blarneyed some American sailors into giving us a bob — five Woodbines and bar of chocolate each. Then home, as the schools were getting out, only to find that Steak Carswell's sister — a girl we called Tombstone Teeth when Steak wasn't about — had told on us. Every one of us got a hiding from our mothers, and the next day we got another one from the master. But it was worth it.

Now, no matter how you look at it, that exploit couldn't be recalled in anything like the same pleasurable way if I was just to use the proper names of all concerned. It would be very plain fare indeed, wouldn't it?

Up Napoleon's Nose

Most Englishmen, when they come to live with us in Northern Ireland, tend to go daft about small boats. Generally speaking, within weeks of their arrival, you couldn't chase them out of the water with gunboats. But not the wife's father. Oh no. When he landed here from London before the war with his wife and Louise — he had to fall in love with the Cave Hill, for heaven's sake.

I put it that way because this hill, to the north of the city, is as familiar to Belfast people as the noses on our faces. And mention of noses brings me to the centre of Roland Miller's love affair with the Cave Hill. For Roland, a true-bred Cockney, was absolutely potty about a twelve hundred foot peak on the hill known locally as Napoleon's Nose. It's called that because, when you turn your head sideways and look at the whole range of hills you see the outline of a very patrician figure, with a huge, hooked nose.

Roland loved this peak so much that he landed his small family into rooms in a house so close to the hill that it very nearly caught the drops from Napoleon's Nose. And he could often be seen standing at the front of this house, looking right up

Napoleon's nostril, heaving great sighs of contentment.

The fact that his landlord, a mercenary and sullen man called Ezekiel Carswell, charged Roland a murderously high rent for the rooms that the three of them occupied made no difference. He was near the Cave Hill: that was enough.

Sunday morning was the time that Roland worshipped at his lofty shrine. He and Louise, a little girl then, would climb the gentle slopes of the hill, drinking in the clean Antrim air, oohing and aahing at the rabbits that were so plentiful on the hill in those days. When Louise grew tired Roland would put her up on to his shoulders, and she would hold him tightly around the neck, resting her chin on his famous peaked cap. This was Roland's old army hat. It had gone through the First World War with him, and he treasured it like an old friend. With its wire rim and badge removed, it gave him quite a piratical look. Louise used to clap her hands with delight when this hat was lifted off its hook at home. It only made its appearance when the hill was to be climbed.

Standing on the grassy bridge of Napoleon's Nose, Roland would look out over the grey-brown expanse of Belfast, lying in its Sunday morning stupor. Underneath the hill the cobbled streets of Tiger's Bay and the New Lodge were ironed flat by the altitude. The black Lagan river coiled like treacle through the city, past the idle gantries of the shipyard: only the bright waters of Belfast Lough were wide awake.

'Cor Blimey,' Roland would say to Louise, 'ain't it lovely?' Standing there on Napoleon's Nose, entranced, he would survey Belfast's numbing drabness: 'There ain't nuffink like this in London,' he would chortle, 'ain't it marvellous?'

But when they got back home again they generally found that Louise's mother Ellen, wasn't all that much interested in the hill. They didn't in the least turn her on. Indeed, as far as Ellen was concerned, a giant moon rock could hurtle out of deep space any time it liked and flatten Napoleon's Nose until it looked more like Jack Dempsey's nose.

No. What worried Ellen Miller was the behaviour of Ezekiel Carswell. In particular she was worried about Ezekiel's treatment of his only child, a quiet fifteen-year old girl called Martha. He never gave Martha an earthly: kept on at her all the time he was in the house. Straighten your shoulders girl. Sit up. Speak up. Don't mumble — that sort of thing.

Martha's mother, Aggie Carswell, had confided to Ellen that Ezekiel's behaviour had come about because of his sudden affluence. He was drinking away beyond his usual quota because of the wealth that Roland's two pounds rent had brought him, and the unfortunate Martha was a sufferer.

The thing came to a head when Martha had her hair bobbed. It had been kept long because Ezekiel wanted it that way, but one day Aggie Carswell had an attack of resolution, got Martha's hair bobbed, and everybody thought it looked a treat.

Everybody but Ezekiel, that is. When he got home from work that night he was furious. So angry was he, in fact, that he ordered Martha to wear a woollen tam o' shanter, indoors and outdoors, until her hair grew long again.

Poor Martha, red-eyed and downcast, retreated

completely within herself. She just sat in the house, staring woodenly at the floor. It was all too much for Roland's wife.

'We've got to go,' she told her husband firmly. 'If Ezekiel Carswell hadn't had the temptation of our rent money, he wouldn't behave like this.'

Roland was appalled. The thought of leaving this house, so near to Napoloeon's Nose, made him feel sick. He decided, therefore, to do something about Ezekiel.

The next Sunday morning dawned bright and clear. Louise, as usual, danced excitedly as the old army hat was lifted off the hook. Off they went, the two of them up the road until they reached the foot of the Cave Hill. Then it was up and away, climbing the green slopes, until they stood triumphantly on Napoleon's Nose. In the old familiar way Roland surveyed, and paid homage to, the sleeping city, then down they went to Ezekiel's house.

The two families were to dine together this Sunday. The others were already seated when Roland walked in. His eye caught Martha's, took in her knitted bonnet, her lifeless features. He winked broadly at her as he took his place at the table and she smiled, her first in two days. For Roland was wearing his old army hat, pulled jauntily over one eye.

'Af'noon,' Roland said cheerily to Ezekiel, 'lovely day for wearing 'ats, i'nt it?' Turning to his wife he jabbed his fork in her direction: 'You're improperly dressed,' he told her.

'Sorry,' said Ellen, with an exaggerated start of surprise. She promptly excused herself to Ezekiel with elaborate politeness. In a few moments she returned: a little red beret was perched cheekily on the back of her head. Now Louise got into the act: she was always quick on the uptake.

'Mummy, Mummy,' she piped up, 'I want to wear my hat too.' At her mother's approving signal Louise ran off to come back soon after, wearing a little tie-on bonnet.

'How nice, dear,' said her mother composedly, helping Roland to cabbage.

Carswell coloured, and muttered beneath his breath, but Roland in this strange mood was too much for him. Meanwhile Roland was making the most outrageously comical faces to Martha until she could keep her gravity no longer. Soon Roland, Louise, Ellen and Martha were roaring with laughter, pointing at each other's hats. It was like Christmas dinner without the crackers and turkey.

In the midst of all this Aggie Carswell had sat mesmerised. Suddenly, without a word, she rose and went into the hall, to return wearing a hat that stepped up the laughter of the others almost to hysteria. Perched on Aggie's head was Ezekiel's black, hard hat, the one he wore for funerals and weddings. She looked like Gertie Gitana, the famous male impersonator of the time.

That did it. Carswell rose from the table and stumped angrily from the room. As he did so Roland reached over and removed Martha's hat.

'It's hats off again,' he said, gently, and the assembled diners swept their hats off too, just to keep Martha company.

But before the afternoon was over Ezekiel had an even bigger surprise waiting for him.

'We're leaving, old cock,' Roland informed him,

as soon as he caught him alone. Ezekiel's face fell. His world had crashed around him today, and no mistake.

'What ... what's the matter?' he asked Roland.

'It's the bloomin' rent,' Roland told him crisply. 'you must take us for bleedin' mugs, or suffink.'

'Is that all?' Carswell said eagerly, 'I'll lower it a bit. How about thirty five bob?' he said anxiously.

'How about a quid, you mean,' Roland suggested, and in the end that was the bargain. Louise and her parents spent another two years with the Carswells, and then they built their own house nearer to Napoleon's Nose, where they lived happily ever after.

I can tell you, without sadness, that today Roland lies in peace, near Black Mountain. He had a good long life and he remained faithful to his true love, the Cave Hill, for many happy years. When Louise and I call to leave him a little bunch of flowers, we always share the thought that no grave in the world could be more exquisitely appropriate than Roland Miller's. He will always and forever lie looking right up Napoleon's Nose...

The Drunken Monk

I suppose it would be as well if I warned you that this story is full of suspense and tension, and the outcome won't become clear until the very end.

It concerns a horse called The Drunken Monk. It was my father who started the whole thing.

Not, mind you, that my father had any interest in the horses. They were light years from *his* mind. Well, how could a merchant seaman keep up an interest in horse racing? For dear sake, once the flat season gets going some of these two year olds are out racing nearly every week trying to get the corn money. During the course of one voyage to the States and back the form of the horses would undergo nothing but one convulsion after another and the whole picture of racing would change totally in between trips home.

So the bookies get very little from merchant seamen. Not but what in 1935 I knew one fireman and trimmer who lost his whole pay-off money at the horses the day he arrived home from a three-month trip. But the punting was very deeply ingrained into this chap: before he went to sea he walked Number Two Blue at Dunmore Park dog track, so it's not surprising that he turned out to be the exception that proves the rule.

My father, when he was at home in the 1930s was perfectly happy to sit in Jimmy McGrane's pub, buying drink for everything that moved, and yarning with his old cronies. But of course, since punting was as much a part of a working man's way of life in those days as going on strike is now, it wasn't surprising that horses should crop up in the conversation. There was my father, and old Hughie Patterson, and Bluenose, a retired seaman, myself, and of course there was Jimmy McGrane leaning over the counter beside us.

'Would you go up to the bookies and put two shillings on The Drunken Monk for me?' old Hughie Patterson asked me. 'Write that down,' he says.

'I don't need to write that down,' I told Hughie. 'The Drunken Monk is well known to me. It couldn't beat my wee sister.'

'Well,' says Hughie Patterson sarcastically, 'since your wee sister's not out at Pontefract today I'll just have to go ahead and back The Drunken Monk, won't I?'

Now my father had come very alert during all this. 'The Drunken Monk,' he repeated, 'that's a great name for a horse.'

'It's a wonder they would allow it,' said Jimmy McGrane. He was very strict about religious matters, Jimmy.

My father shoved his two fingers into his waistcoat pocket and produced a pound note. 'Put that on The Drunken Monk,' he said, 'I've a feeling it's a winner.'

'If you don't mind me saying so,' I told him,

that's the sort of feeling that has led a good many non-swimmers to dive off bridges.'

With that old Bluenose came alive. 'Put that five bob on for me,,' he says, and then I'm jiggered if Jimmy McGrane didn't get caught up in the excitement and throw a pound note into the pile as well.

There was only five minutes to the off, so away I went with the money, feeling rather depressed at such a waste. On the way I ran into Fat Carson and started telling him about it.

'Lay it yourself,' he said. 'The Drunken Monk couldn't win in a walkover with an outboard motor strapped on to his behind.' I hurried away from the temptation, and this is where the horror starts.

For the race was off just as I went through the door of the bookies. 'They're off at Pontefract,' said the loudspeaker and the wee wooden shutter came down so fast that it nearly nipped the fingers off me.

I rapped the shutter with a two bob bit. 'Let me on,' I shouted anxiously, 'forty seven shillings straight on The Drunken Monk.'

'You're too late,' this voice says, 'they're off at Pontefract.'

'Well this is Belfast,' I shouts, 'what kind of risk are you taking in letting me on?'

'Go away,' this voice says. 'I'm busy.'

Heavens above and the earth beneath, I said to myself. This is the one time that The Drunken Monk'll hack up as round as a hoop. If it wins, says I in desperation, I'll have to seek the sanctuary of some church. The Drunken Monk was twenty to one in betting, you see.

Just with that the loudspeaker starts up. 'Result

'It was second,' I said.

at Pontefract,' it says. 'Number Eight, Brasso, the winner. Number Fourteen, The Drunken Monk, second.'

You talk about a sigh of relief. I just went limp, like a piece of wet string. But before I could properly enjoy the sensation up crackles the loudspeaker again: 'There's an objection to the winner at Pontefract,' the loudspeaker announces.

Well I'm telling you, in the space of one second I was transformed into a craven, trembling wreck. I wasn't even able to wait there in the bookies for the outcome. I rushed blindly out into Halliday's Road.

'Isn't that a beautiful afternoon,' some clergyman said, going past.

'Oh it is,' says I, 'perfectly smashing' — and I hope says I to myself, you trip going up the steps to the pulpit.

Fifteen agonising minutes later I walked into the pub. 'Well,' they all said together, eagerly.

'It was second,' I said, 'but there was an objection to the winner.'

'Well hurry up,' they all shouted, 'did it win the objection?'

'It was overruled,' I told them, 'didn't I tell you it was a donkey?'

'Now,' I said to Jimmy McGrane, putting forty seven shillings on the counter, 'hit these men with half 'uns of whiskey till The Drunken Monk is nothing but a faint memory.'

Carrickfergus Castle — The Truth

Carrickfergus Castle's a very famous place, isn't it? Well then, tell me one thing: why is it that you never read about my Uncle Alec in any of the books or articles that are written about it, eh?

De Courcy's mentioned all right, and Essex. Sorley Boy MacDonnell as well. That's all right: they deserve to be. But so does my Uncle Alec. And where's his name? I'll tell you where it is — it's nowhere, that's where it is.

Well I'm about to put the record straight. OK?

My Uncle Alec was involved in World War One but he didn't fancy the army a bit. He tended to go and get drunk instead of going on parade and the army doesn't permit that, so things didn't go too hotsy totsy for him. My Uncle Alec's father, who was a committed member of the Communist party, told him to take his medicine like a man.

'Obey your orders,' he said, 'and learn to shoot a rifle. You'll need it against the employing classes soon.'

So my Uncle Alec accepted his punishment, and mind you it was no joke. Over in France when you went out and got full drunk instead of going on parade you were tied to a wheel, that's what

Imagine having a hangover tied to a wheel.

happened to you. The wheel of a gun carriage. Imagine having a hangover tied to a wheel! It happened to my Uncle Alec about four times. The people who owned the vineyards should have given him the Croix de Guerre for devotion to drinking.

Anyway, in God's good time they put him in the trenches. Some officer blows a whistle and shouts 'Charge!' Up they go and over the top. Ten yards my Uncle Alec runs and then he goes down like a hundredweight of spuds. Three holes in him.

They took him to the field hospital, then the base hospital, then they sent him home for a fortnight's sick leave. Then they ordered him back to the trenches.

'Don't aim at the Germans,' his father advised him, 'they're workers like us. But if you see any employers of labour about,' he finished hopefully, 'aim at them all right.'

Well, the whole thing was academic. Into the trenches. Officer blows the whistle: 'Charge!' Climb the ladder, charge like anything. Fifteen yards. Hundredweight of spuds. Two more holes in him.

Field hospital, base hospital, two weeks' sick leave.

The fates conspired against him. The day before he was due to go back to join his regiment he gets a treble up at the horses. Six quid. He got poleaxed for two more days, as anybody would.

The Redcaps lifted him as he was sitting in the house getting dug into a pig's knee. He was charged the same day and got twenty one days detention for whilst on active service being absent without leave.

And now we're coming to the crux of the whole thing. For where did the army shove my Uncle Alec to do his twenty one days? Right first time. Carrickfergus Castle, well-known British army garrison, built in the Twelfth Century, and crammed full of people like my Uncle Alec for most of the time ever since.

He went into the dungeons every night. During the day he got pack drill and running on the spot. He also had to whitewash the coal bunker till it looked like alabaster. Then the corporal threw all the coal back into it and complained because it was filthy.

But one thing held him together during his ordeal: the thought of his shilling a day wages building up for him. With the pint at threepence that made eighty four pints. Good incentive for any prisoner, you'll understand.

On the last day of his sentence he's lined up with the others due for release. An officer sitting at a table calls out my Uncle Alec's name.

'Sir,' he shouts eagerly.

'One and ninepence,' the officer says, in a bored voice.

'You head's cut,' my Uncle Alec tells him, 'it's twenty one shillings.'

'You are only entitled to one penny per day whilst in prison, my man,' the officer says, 'that comes to one and ninepence. Now pick up your pay and go.'

'Oh, so that's the way of it,' my Uncle Alec replies. 'Well, if I was you I would watch what I was saying.'

'Are you threatening me?' the officer says, with his eyebrows up in his hair.

'Too Irish I am,' my Uncle Alec shouts, and with

that he flattens a nearby sergeant, grabs the table, and upends the officer, money, papers and everything. 'How's that for a penny's worth,' my Uncle Alec yells, as they drag him to the dungeons for practically the rest of the war.

So there you are. That's my Uncle Alec's story for you. He was a good 'un, wasn't he?

I'll tell you this much: I reckon he was as good a man for the history books as that de Courcy, or Essex, or any of that lot. You never heard tell of any of them putting an officer on his backside, did you?

Do you see these history books? It's not what you know — it's who you know.

A Pound of Steak for Stuffing

I was sitting around the house tending to get in under the sister's feet, and, more to get rid of me than anything else, she asked me would I go round to Joe O'Neill's in Duncairn Gardens and get a pound of steak for stuffing. Right, says I, no bother at all.

It was 1946, and me and thousands more like me were just out of the forces, and in no great notion of working.

'Where are you heading?' Sammy Coleman wanted to know. He was holding up the wall at the corner of Lepper Street.

'I've to go to the butcher's for a pound of steak for stuffing,' I told him. He levered himself off the wall to come with me.

Reaching the Duncairn Gardens, who's standing on the far whack waiting for a tram but Jimmy Armstrong, one-time barman, now unemployed tank driver. 'Where are you for?' we asked him. He looked embarrassed and beckoned us across the road.

'I'm for Dublin,' he explained, when we reached him, 'it's the woman. She's not writing.'

We remembered the snaps of the Free Stater he'd

shown us in McGrane's pub. They'd met in England when he was getting demobbed from the Army.

Just with that his tram appeared. 'What about leaving him to the station?' Sammy Coleman suggested.

'You're on,' says I, putting my foot on the tram.

'Service,' says Sammy to the conductor, getting a free ride. He learned this trick from a guy whose brother was on the buses. Some day you'll get caught on at that, we told him. He didn't even look like a bus conductor.

Down in Robinson's bar, with three quarters of an hour before Jimmy got his train, I hurried up and got the pints in. I'd no sooner put them on the table than in walks Jackie Black.

'Where were you this last six and a half years?' we all asked him. It turned out he'd been very unhappy and ill-adjusted on destroyers.

'What are you doing here?' we quizzed him next, knowing he didn't live too far from ourselves. He was on his way to put a deposit on a fireplace for his mother, it seemed.

Inside the next forty minutes we hoovered up five pints each. It didn't seem an outlandish proposal, therefore, when Jackie Black says what about all going to Dublin, boys, and coming back tomorrow. On we trooped to the Dublin train, trekking through the carriage to locate the bar.

Spotting a group of clergy in one of the carriages, Sammy Coleman makes a trumpet out of his hand and shouts: 'Is there a clergyman on the train, please?'

Of course, as one, they all looked up, hoping to hear tell of somebody trapped under the wheels or something. Once he had their undivided attention, Sammy puts his hands to his mouth again: 'We're looking for a corkscrew,' he shouts. 'Any clergymen on the train?' He was dynamite, Sammy.

We spent nearly the entire journey standing in the bar having fun with a Free Stater, who told us within the first seconds of meeting him that he had been at the Normandy do with the artillery. We were all letting on we were munitions workers during the war.

'Did it not make you feel awfully soiled, sleeping on the ground, and everything?' Jimmy Armstrong asked. He himself had spent the war sleeping under tanks. The Free Stater told us you get used to it.

'Does the shell of a gun work the same as a bullet?' Jackie Black enquired. 'I mean, does it have to get hit on the bottom with a kind of a spikey thing?'

'Well, actually,' the Free Stater told him, 'you'd be surprised how near the truth you are,' and he explained it to us.

'It must have been appallingly embarrassing for you, sometimes,' I put in. 'I believe some of those uncouth sergeants asked you to report to the doctor with slacks at the slope.'

The Free Stater looked at me a bit suspiciously, then his face cleared and he told us the joke about the lady Army doctor, and the private stripped to the pelt who couldn't stop himself from signalling his admiration for her. 'She put him on a charge for dumb insolence,' the Free Stater finished, and we all fell about helplessly laughing, although we'd heard it about fifty thousand times apiece.

Tumbling out of the train in Amiens Street

station we bade the Free Stater all the best.

'You've impressed me so much with your clean cutness,' Jackie Black told him, 'that I'm going straight to Clifton Street to join the artillery, just as soon as ever I get back to Belfast.' He looked at the rest of us with eyes glowing. 'Anybody care to join me?' he asked.

'Too Irish!' we chorused. 'I'd like to see who's going to stop us.'

'You three might think you've wiped that Free Stater's eye,' I reminded the others, as we waved bye bye enthusiastically to him, 'but the truth of the matter is — he never bought a drink during that whole trip.'

The next thing was, what about accommodation. We looked hopefully at Jimmy Armstrong. 'You can't stop in my woman's house, anyway,' Jimmy said, quickly. 'I can't afford to be diverted, for I think I've got a problem on my hands.'

'Is that what's on your hands?' Sammy remarked. 'I was wondering what it was.' The drink was taking a grip of him.

We wished Jimmy Armstrong all the best and headed on into Dublin, eventually getting into a hotel near St Stephen's Green. A good scrub down, a feed of bacon, eggs, sausage and black pudding, and we were ready to greet the city of Dublin properly.

'You'll need to watch yourselves, boys,' warned a little man who had chummed up with us in Mooney's, 'Dublin's full of fruits.' As he spoke he tapped Jackie Black's knee earnestly.

We looked at one another. 'Did I not meet you in Cairo, in '42?' Sammy Coleman asked him, sounding like one himself. 'D'ye not mind you an' me admiring the big hairy barman?' Our new friend shimmied off, disappointedly.

We discovered a small dance with a bar at one end. Within minutes Sammy Coleman was off his mark with a PT teacher. He told her he'd been half-mile champion of the Royal Air Force.

'What an immense relief to find a kindred spirit,' she said, 'Mens corpore mens sana,' she added.

'No,' Sammy explained, 'I wasn't a corporal — I was a flight sergeant.'

'Healthy mind, healthy body,' the skirt said and we all looked at her body with healthy respect. In no time at all Sammy Coleman and her was offside, Sammy having expressed a desire to see her barbells. That left Jackie Black and me.

Next thing who turns up there in Dublin but Aggie Quinn from Lewis Street, just beside us at home. From the outset it was clear that she was looking to Jackie Black to lighten her darkness, and not me. Straightening his tie and combing his hair, Jackie suggested a pastie supper.

'I hope I didn't come all the way to Dublin with my married sister just to end up with a pastie supper,' Aggie says, on her dignity.

'If you walk out of that door with Jackie Black,' I said, earnestly, 'you'll definitely end up with more than a pastie supper.' Away the two of them went, leaving only me, but already I had my quarry marked out.

She was small, but well upholstered. She was sitting with a long, toothy girl friend at a nearby table. Morse code messages had been flashing between us for a long enough time for me to make a move, I got her up on the floor.

'Where did you learn to dance?' she asked pertly. 'On the football field?'

'My dear young lady,' I said, 'Belfast is renowned the world over for the standard of its dancers. Yet,' I continued, slewing her round in my usual half-nelson reverse turn, 'I am in constant demand in each and every dance hall in that fair and graceful city.'

'Don't try to tell me you're a professional dancer,' she said, coyly.

'No,' I replied, roaring at my own joke, 'I'm the man that sells the pigs' feet.'

After the dance I joined her at the table, sitting opposite Fangs, her mate. Soon afterwards we were joined by a guy who wasn't long home after being in a Japanese prison camp. Hardly able to believe her luck, Fangs hurried him off outside before his eyesight returned to normal.

'Can I leave you home?' I asked Alma, the wee one.

'You've talked me into it,' she says. She lived in a house not far from the city centre. It was all in darkness when we got there.

'Shush,' she says, as she opened the parlour door, 'me da's good livin'.'

'Lush,' says I to myself, knowing the hot orders of daughters that good-living das turn out.

I was right. In no time she was on to me like a giant anaconda.

'What about yer da?' I said, more for something to say while I was trying to work out the combination for her blouse. Suddenly the lights blazed on.

'Aye — what about her da!' says this guy who

looks like King Kong with the earache. He had hands like shovels. He didn't believe me when I tried to explain that his daughter had been knocked down by a bicycle and I had brought her in for rest and recuperation. He caught me a looter on the ear and another one on the eye, before I managed to hit the street, running.

Back in the hotel, I fell across the bed and slept for six hours. Sammy Coleman and Jackie Black woke me up. 'The train'll be going soon,' they said.

Jackie Black had lost his jacket. Aggie Quinn had taken a fancy to a Kerry man in the chip shop, and Jackie threw the coat off to him. He got knocked out and his coat got knocked off.

Sammy Coleman had a sore leg. The PT teacher's brother had thrown him down the stairs after proving him a liar about being the half-mile champion.

'I got mixed up,' Sammy explained. 'I told them I did the half mile in fifteen minutes.'

Jimmy Armstrong was at the station looking glum. His woman had beetled off with a scaffolder from Terenure two days earlier. Jimmy had spent some time at the zoo, considering whether to feed himself to the lions or not. But in the end he got drunk with a communist and ended up giving nearly all his money to the Party.

We cured our heads in the train going home. When we landed in Belfast we went our separate ways, and wished each other all the best.

'Give us a pound of steak for stuffing,' I said to Joe O'Neill.

'Where did you get the black eye?' he asked me, as he was slicing the steak.

'On a sofa in Dublin,' I told him. You could see he didn't believe me.

'Did you get the pound of steak for stuffing?' the sister called out from the kitchen, when I opened the door wearily. 'I did,' says I.

'You took your time about it,' she sniffed.